Lear

The Beginners Guide for Learning Piano

The Guide to Learn Piano like a Pro

By: Margo Chen

ISBN No. 978-1631874680

The Excellent Guide of Learning Piano

TABLE OF CONTENTS

Publishers Notes 4

Dedication 5

Chapter 1- The Main Reason Anyone Should Play Piano 6

    Familiarizing Piano 7

    Learning A to G Home Keys 9

Chapter 2- All About Keys 12

    Learning To Read Music 14

    Reading Lines and Spaces 15

    Coordination of Notes and Rhythm 18

Chapter 3- Narrative Encouragement 21

    Key Signature Holds the Key 22

    Learning about Chords 24

Chapter 4- Understanding Chords and modification 27

    Playing Music for the first time by Sight Reading 28

Chapter 5- Piano Language and Terminology 31

    Choosing Music that is Right for You 33

Chapter 6- Practice makes perfect 36

    Playing Piano for Everyone 37

    Playing for the Public 39

Chapter 7- Inspiring Personal Stories 41

Chapter 8- Tips in Playing Piano for Beginners.................................. 43

    Piano Lessons and Mentor.. 44

Chapter 9- Learning and Enjoying For a Lifetime........................... 47

About The Author... 49

PUBLISHERS NOTES
Disclaimer

This publication is intended to provide helpful and informative material. The author and publisher specifically disclaim all responsibility for any liability, loss or risk, personal or otherwise, which is incurred as a consequence, directly or indirectly, from the use or application of any contents of this book.

Any and all product names referenced within this book are the trademarks of their respective owners. None of these owners have sponsored, authorized, endorsed, or approved this book.

Always read all information provided by the manufacturers' product labels before using their products. The author and publisher are not responsible for claims made by manufacturers.

Paperback Reprint Edition

Spirala Publishing

contact@spiralaPublishing.com

www.spiralaPublishing.com

Distributed by:

Speedy Publishing LLC
40 E. Main St. #1156
Newark, DE 19711
www.speedypublishing.co

Manufactured in the United States of America

DEDICATION

I dedicate this book to my Dad Jason Chen who is a very supportive and a loving father. To my Mom who is my personal inspiration to strive, learn, and achieve more. I also dedicate this book to all of the children who want to learn fast learning piano lessons. This is the right book for you, very simple, straight forward and will absolutely provide quality learning.

Chapter 1 - The Main Reason Anyone Should Play Piano

You probably already know that piano playing is an exciting talent to develop. If you are a jazz enthusiast, you may have listened to piano music from great artists like Count Basie or Duke Ellington. You might like modern jazz piano players better and there are many who have won the hearts of audiences everywhere.

One piano player who crosses many genres is Jim Brickman, who often plays his own compositions. Along with smooth jazz stations, Brickman's music is played on pop, inspirational, and new age stations.

You may be more interested in the rock keyboard players. Some of them have been: Rick Wakeman of Yes, Tony Banks of Genesis, Dennis De Young of Styx, and David Sancious who played for Springsteen, Santana, and Sting. Rock piano players include Elton John, Billy Joel, Carole King, Paul McCartney, and Carly Simon.

Even if you have never liked classical music before, you might begin to enjoy it once you have started to play the piano. It presents a challenge and is very satisfying to master. Some of the greats are Bach, Beethoven, Mendelssohn, Schubert, and Brahms.

If you are like many people who hear these great musical works of art, you will want to emulate them. You may learn well enough to play for a band or as a solo act if you are dedicated enough. You can certainly learn to play the piano well enough to entertain yourself, your friends, and your family.

There are other benefits to playing the piano as well. One is relaxation. When you feel upset, it is very therapeutic to play the piano for awhile. If you are angry, playing the piano can release your frustrations. Your playing will soothe your nerves if you are anxious. If you are feeling down, you can start with slow songs and build up to more up-tempo, happier-sounding songs. This will often lift your sad mood.

If you do end up playing professionally, you can gain a source of income from your piano playing. Some piano players earn very little – just some tips from a jar on their piano bar instrument. Other piano players can earn fantastic amounts of money if they are talented enough and lucky enough.

Another reason to learn to play piano is to develop discipline. If you are someone who starts and stops activities without giving them a fair shot, you might have better luck with the piano. It gives rewards at every level, keeping you motivated to stay at it and work harder.

Learning to play the piano is easier in some ways than learning other types of music. With vocal music, you have to learn more carefully about pitch. You have to worry about being just a touch above or below the note. With a piano, the only way that would happen is if your piano is out of tune, in which case you just have a technician fix it.

The main reason anyone should learn to play the piano is for their own fulfillment. No matter what that means to you, you will be happy when you have strived to reach your full potential. You will feel joy when you play a composition well. You will be a happier person for letting music into your life.

Familiarizing Piano

Before you begin to play the piano, you need to become familiar with what the instrument is. Some pianos are upright pianos, which are usually large, heavy, tall vertical boxes. These are anywhere from 36 to 51 inches tall. Spinets are the shortest upright pianos, at 36 to 39 inches. A studio vertical is 44 inches or taller.

The Excellent Guide of Learning Piano

If you have the opportunity to play on a grand piano, you will usually get a better sound and a more responsive touch. Grand pianos are the more horizontal pianos, ranging from 5 to 9 feet in length. In a grand piano, the strings are horizontal. In a vertical piano, the strings are, well, vertical.

The piano will have a music rack of some kind where you can put your sheet music. It may fold down or slide into a slot. When you are ready to play, put it into position. There should also be a bench for you to sit on. Adjust the position of the bench so that you can reach all the keys from one end of the keyboard to the other. Do not sit either too far or away or too close.

There will be pedals at the bottom of the piano where your feet are. These need not be used by beginners. Once you become more proficient at playing the piano, you can learn how to use these pedals to sustain sounds or cut them short.

The part of the piano that will be most important to your learning is the keyboard. It is made up of white and black keys which run from the left to the right of the piano face. These keys do not alternate white-black-white for the entire length of the keyboard.

If you look closely, you will see that the black and white keys form a pattern that repeats from one end of the keyboard to the other. The pattern consists of 7 white keys and 5 black keys in a particular order. From the beginning of one such set of keys and ending on the beginning of the next set, an interval is formed. Intervals are just the musical distances between two sounds. This particular interval is called an octave.

The keys are lined up on the keyboard in order from the lowest on the left to the highest on the right. Starting at the left and moving to the right, each black or white key is a half step higher in pitch than the key before it. For a full step, it is necessary to go up (or down) two half steps. Try some half steps and some full steps. With a little practice, you should be able to learn the sound of those intervals easily.

Try other intervals to hear their sounds. Always pay attention to how many half or full steps you are taking. Do the same intervals at several different places along the keyboard. Try octaves. You can do this by picking out a key and playing the next key up that is in the same position in the next pattern group. Soon, you will be playing octaves with ease. This is very important to all kinds of piano playing.

Now that you have familiarized yourself with the instrument called the piano, you can begin to learn how to use it to make music. There is much to learn, but you can begin playing simple songs very quickly. All it takes is a little time and some effort, and soon you will be happily playing songs you enjoy. What starts with a few notes can end in a lifelong pursuit of musical accomplishment.

LEARNING A TO G HOME KEYS

You can start by learning where to put your hands. There are a group of keys toward the center of the keyboard called the Home Keys. These are nine keys where your hands should rest as you prepare to play.

You might wonder why there are only nine Home Keys when you have ten fingers. The reason is that both thumbs rest on middle C. Middle C is a reference point that will be referred to over and over as you are learning and studying the piano. It can be recognized by looking at the pattern of black and white keys at the center of the keyboard. Look at the picture of the center of a piano keyboard below. Take notice of the keys that do not have a black key to separate them. This is how you recognize the pattern.

5   4   3   2   C   2   3   4   5

--Figure A--

The middle C, where you will put your thumbs, is marked with a C. The keys with numbers under them are where you put your fingers. The twos are for the index fingers of your left and right hand, the threes are for your middle fingers, the fours are for your ring fingers, and the fives are for your little fingers.

Place your fingers on the Home Keys of your piano keyboard. Play to the right up the keyboard from your right thumb to your right little finger. Now play down the keyboard from your left thumb to your left little finger.

You can even play a few songs with your hands in the Home Keys position. Try to pick out a song you know well. For example, you can play Mary Had a Little Lamb with the right hand when it is in the Home Keys position. Try to use your memory of the sounds to choose the right keys. (Hint: start with your right middle finger.)

Now, try using the Home Keys for a reference point. Put your fingers on the Home Keys again. Look up the keyboard, to the right, for the next pattern that looks just like the Home Keys. You know where middle C is – now try to find the C of the next octave up. Look from middle C to the C above middle C. This is how you will gauge your place on the keyboard.

In the beginning, you should always take a long look at the keyboard when you sit down to play. Once you can recognize the home keys, you can begin any song from that reference point. When you have learned more, you will take one glance at middle C and know exactly where to put your fingers no matter where they should go up or down the keyboard.

Next you need to learn the names of the keys, A through G. You know where middle C is now. Start two white keys below that and you will be at A. Each white key up, or to the right, goes up a letter in the alphabet until you come to G. Then, it starts over at A.

Therefore, the middle finger of your left hand is resting on the A in the Home Keys position. As you go to the right, you will reach G by the time you get to the little finger of your right hand.

So, what are the black keys for? They are just as important. They represent the sharps or flats. Interestingly enough, the same key can be either a sharp or a flat. When you go up from a white key, the black key is a sharp, and when you go down from a white key, the black key is a flat.

To try an example, go again to middle C. Go up to the black key to the right of middle C. This is C sharp. Now, move one white key up, to the index finger of your right hand. This is a D. Go to the black key to the left of D. This is D flat. Amazing, isn't it? C sharp and D flat are both represented by the same key on the piano.

As you learn more, you will discover that both the black keys and the white keys are equally important in piano music. There would be few opportunities to have half steps on the piano without black keys, and most songs have some half steps in them. Also, there are many instances where the black keys are some of the main keys in the predominant scale being used.

CHAPTER 2- ALL ABOUT KEYS

A scale goes from one key to the key that is an octave above that key. It consists of eight tones. There are different types of scales. Some of them are major scales and some of them are minor scales. Major scales have been described as sounding happy, while minor scales are said to sound sad or gloomy.

If you spend a part of your practice time playing scales, you build muscle memory in your hands. This means that, after much time practicing, your hands go more easily to notes in the scale you are playing at any given time. You only have to see the printed music or think of the melody and your hands know what to do.

To talk about scales, you must talk about keys. There are two kinds of keys when you are learning to play the piano. There are the physical blocks of ivory, or some look-alike material, and wood. There are also keys that scales or songs are played in.

Have you ever been to a lounge where a singer is giving an impromptu performance? She might lean down to the pianist and say something like, "In the key of C." That tells the pianist where on the keyboard to begin. It also tells the pianist what physical keys to start with and what chords to use. The key of a piece of music is very important.

When you are learning scales, you can do it without learning all the key signatures. (Key signatures are the written notation of the keys, such as the key of C or the key of G.) You can begin by playing a C scale. A major C scale is all done on the white keys. Begin with your right hand in the Home Keys position. Remember that your fingers are numbered 1-5, with the thumb being 1.

Play 1-2-3 as usual. This is C-D-E on the keyboard. Then, instead of playing the next note with your ring finger, slip your thumb under the fingers and play F with your thumb. Reposition your hand so that your thumb is 1 on F and your pinkie is 5 on the C above middle C. Then, continue to play up the scale. So, you are playing 1-2-3-1-2-3-4-5, or C-D-E-F-G-A-B-C. You have just played your first scale. Practice it a few times.

To play a C scale with your left hand, put your little finger on the C below middle C. Position your fingers from 1-5 coming up the keyboard from each key to the next. Play 5-4-3-2-1. Then, reach over the top with your middle finger and place it on the next key. Play 3-2-1 from this position. Therefore, you are playing 5-4-3-2-1-3-2-1, or C-D-E-F-G-A-B-C.

After you practice this for awhile, try to put the left hand and the right hand together. Play the C below middle C with your left pinkie at the same time as you play the middle C with your left thumb. Continue up the scale with both hands. It can be a little tricky at first because you are going over with your middle finger of your left hand and the under with the thumb of the right hand at different times. Practice awhile and it will come naturally.

Once you get the basic procedure down, it is easy to play other major scales. The only thing you have to remember is the sequence of steps and half steps in a major scale. The correct order up a major scale is: beginning note-step-step-half step-step-step-step-half step. You should be aware that, since there are no black keys between them, the intervals from B-C and from E-F are each half steps.

You can play a scale anywhere on the piano. Just pick a note to start on. It does not matter whether it is a white key or a black key. Use the given sequence of steps and half steps to go from there up an eight note scale. You can even start from the left of the keyboard and continue the scale all the way to the right. With a little practice, you will be proficient at playing major scales.

Learning To Read Music

With a little success under your belt, you can begin to tackle the job of learning to read music. Of course, many musicians do not know how to read music. They just hear a song and play it, as they say, by ear. These musicians can improvise on any simple themes and come up with elaborate renditions of popular songs. These players know their instruments as well as singers know their own voices.

You may be someone who can do that. There will be some information later on about chords and improvisation. However, if you are a beginner just finding out about the piano, it is more likely that you need the help that written music can provide you. Furthermore, learning to read written music can open up a whole new world to you. You can learn songs that you have never even heard before. If you want to repeat the performance, you will have the sheet music to guide you note for note.

There is much to learn. You must find out about the way the notes are depicted. You need to know what the staffs that they are shown on look like. You will learn how rhythm is represented and how sharps and flats are shown. These are the basics, and you can build on this knowledge over time.

You can learn quite a lot just by looking at one piece of music. If you have some sheet music, a hymnal, or a songbook, take it out and look at the music. If you do not already have some written music, buy some or borrow a songbook from the library.

You will notice that there are groups of five horizontal lines. If the music is for both hands, it will have two of these groups of lines connected together by a longer line along the side. The horizontal lines are called the staff. You can get staff paper that is already marked with these lines.

Margo Chen

At the far left side of the staffs you will see the clef marking. It will be a treble clef marking for the upper staff. The treble clef resembles a fancy backwards S with a line going down through it and curling underneath. In the beginning of learning to play the piano, you will play the treble clef notes with your right hand.

On the lower staff of the two is the bass clef sign. It is something like a backwards C with two dots on the right side of it. This staff shows the lower notes, and you will begin by playing the notes shown on this staff with your left hand. The upper and lower staffs will repeat several times down the page. Look at your sheet music and identify the staffs. Now you are ready to learn the notes.

READING LINES AND SPACES

Your first experience with playing music from written notations will come as soon as you learn the notes. The first thing you have to do is to learn about the lines and the spaces of the staffs. On the diagram below, the notes used are all quarter notes. That refers to the rhythm of the notes which will be discussed later. The purpose of this diagram is to show you the notes as they are positioned on the staff.

Treble   C   D   E   F   G   A   B   C   D   E   F

--Figure B--

If you look just at the actual lines of the staff, you will see that they are, going up, E-G-B-D-F. Some people remember this with little sayings, like "Every Good Boy Does Fine." There are memory tricks for all the lines and spaces on both staffs. For the spaces of the treble clef, you will notice that the letters of the notes spell F-A-C-E.

Now, you can relate the notes on the page to the keys on the keyboard. Remember where the middle C is? The C on the left of the diagram above depicts middle C. The middle C is shown on an added line below the treble clef or above the bass clef. Using middle C as a reference point and your new knowledge of the letters that go with the notes, try to look at each note and then play the key it refers to.

Take the music you have at hand, and try to pick out a few notes on the piano from the treble clef. You might even be able to play a melody line by using this method. This will only get you started. However, every time you can have the satisfying experience of playing music, you should take it. The feeling will carry you on to want to learn more.

There are more notes to learn on the bass clef. A diagram of the bass clef with the notes on the lines and spaces is shown below.

Bass   G   A   B   C   D   E   F   G   A   B   C

--Figure C--

On this diagram, the middle C is shown on the far right, which would be the end of this short piece of music. The lines of the bass clef are G-B-D-F-A. Many people turn the treble clef saying around and use the saying "Good Boys Do Fine Always." The spaces are A-C-E-G. One popular mnemonic device for this is, "All Cows Eat Grass." Feel free to make up anything that will help you to remember. Write your sayings down and memorize them.

Another thing to learn is the notation for sharps and flats. This is the sign for a sharp: #. It is placed to the left of the note. The flat is a totally different sign. It looks something like a small letter b that has been squeezed until the circle looks almost like a half of a heart shape. It is also put on the left side of a note. Look through your printed music for any sharps and flats you might recognize.

Do not worry about the rhythm at this point. Take your written music and play as many notes as you can from it. Say the note names as you play at first. This will get you in the habit of thinking about the written note as a musical sound with a letter name. Associating the three aspects of a note together will help you become more proficient at reading music.

Buy some staff paper or make your own. You can make staff paper by drawing five straight horizontal lines across the page, leaving a space, and then drawing five more horizontal lines. Now you can draw some notes to play simple strings of notes.

Draw a note by making a filled in circle either on a line or in a space. Then, draw a line up from it on the right. Make notes on different lines and in different spaces. Set aside your pencil and try playing your notes. You should be able to look at the note you have drawn and think of the letter name and the physical piano key it belongs to. Pretty soon, you will be playing all the notes you can write. If it comes naturally to you, you might start coming up with music you enjoy listening to as you write your notes.

When you have learned all about the lines and spaces, you will be well on your way to understanding written music. The next step is to understand how chords are written. Chords are notes that are played simultaneously.

You will recognize chords on the sheet music because they are written in a vertical line. If they are quarter notes, as the notes in the previous diagrams are, they will share the line that goes along the side of the note. There will be more on chords later. For now, just take a look at how they are shown.

Try to play some chords as they are on your written music. You may have to place one finger on a note at a time when you are first learning, but eventually you will see the chord and your fingers will go into that position. Do a little practice with chords and get ready to learn about rhythm.

COORDINATION OF NOTES AND RHYTHM

Rhythm is something that can be improvised or changed easily if you know the piano well. Think about singing: You can sing by holding some notes longer and cutting other notes shorter. You do not need to be told how to do it.

If you want to learn a song that you do not know, written music can be used to help you understand the rhythm. Also, if you want to play in an ensemble that is playing from sheet music, you will stay in time with them better if you play from written music as well.

The first thing you need to learn about rhythm is the time signatures. The time signature is written to the right of the treble and bass clefs on the first line of a piece of music. If the time signature changes within the piece, a different set of numbers is written at the point where the change is about to take place.

A time signature is two numbers, one over the other. The top number tells you how many beats there are to a measure. A measure is a unit of the musical piece that is marked off by a vertical line through the staff. There should be identical vertical lines through the treble and bass staffs at various points. Try to find them on your music.

The bottom number tells you what kind of note makes one beat. Therefore, a 3/4 time signature would mean that there are three notes to a measure and these notes are quarter notes. As you become more familiar with piano rhythms, you will see that the time signatures are more of a suggestion than an order to stamp your foot and play a quarter note with each beat. However, to begin it is easiest if you do if you tap your foot and play one beat per every note of the type listed in the bottom of the time signature.

Notes have different values based upon how they are written. A whole note is the basis of the rhythm. A measure can consist of a whole note and nothing more. In 4/4 time, a whole note is worth 4 beats. This makes sense when you consider that a quarter note is worth 1 beat. 4 quarter notes would make one measure. Four fourths equals a whole.

Music rhythm is very similar to math. In fact, it has been shown in studies that babies who are exposed to hearing music with complex rhythms are better at complex math later in life. To begin, though, you only need to know a few simple equations.

If a whole note is worth 4 quarter notes, it can be worth two half notes as well. A measure can also be divided up into eighth notes. A whole note, two half notes, or four quarter notes are worth eight eighth notes. When you add a dot to a note, it adds half again to that note. So, a dotted half note would be worth three beats, or the duration of three quarter notes.

The whole note is a simple circle with an open center. The half note is the same, but it has a line coming up from the side of it, making it look different. The quarter note is like the half note, except that the center of the circle is filled in. An eighth note has a small flag on the line coming up from the note. It can look like this if it is alone: ♪. Or it can look like this if it is with another eighth note: ♫.

Look at your sheet music and identify the note values. To practice, tap your foot to establish the baseline rhythm. It should be a steady beat. Clap your hands to the rhythm of the note values. If it is a whole note, clap once and then do not clap again until you have tapped your foot three more times. If it is two eighth notes, clap once as you put your foot down and another time as you pick your foot up.

Try clapping out rhythms of any sheet music you can get your hands on. Often there will be more than one simple line of music, so you must choose to ignore all but one line to begin. Clap out one note at a time, which is the only way you could do it anyway.

The Excellent Guide of Learning Piano

When you are good at clapping out rhythms, go on to playing notes in rhythm. If you cannot find music that is simple enough for you to understand, make up some of your own. Use the staff paper you have purchased or made. Make a 4/4 time signature and write some measures. Make sure you always put in notes that add up to 4 beats, or one whole note. You can also use rests, which are notations denoting a pause where nothing is played at all on that clef.

You can play your composition from your sheet. It may not sound like a song to you, but the rhythm will be interesting if you have used different note values. It is fun to make up your own music.

You can use this method to practice the particular aspects of music you are learning. When you do, you are not forced to search for music that fits the situation. At the same time, you are practicing coming up with examples of concepts you are trying to learn. It trains your mind. All along, you can also be testing out what you have learned by trying to play parts of written music that you have on hand. It can all be a part of the process.

Chapter 3 - Narrative Encouragement

I was one of those people who always dreamed of playing the piano but never thought I could. At least I was until I came across some short, simple lessons on the basics of piano playing. I decided to give it a try, and I have been practicing ever since.

When I started, I knew what a piano looked like, but I had not really taken notice of how the white and black keys make a pattern. That was the first little bit of instruction that helped me to realize that the piano might be decipherable after all. Since the keyboard could be broken down into sections, I had something to guide me in finding each individual key.

I began with the lessons that were in the material I had. After each section, I had to try out the concepts I had found out about. I had to try to play the notes, write the notes, clap the rhythms, or play lines of melody. In awhile, I began to test myself. I went back over the lessons and tried each concept. I did this several times, always getting better and better.

I developed my own practice schedule, finding time between my work and daily chores. It was satisfying to accomplish so much so quickly. The slow pace of formal lessons may be good for children, but as an adult, I appreciated the ability to go at my own pace.

There came a time when I wanted to play music that was easy for me – music that I recognized rather than what I was writing out in my exercises. So, I went to the music store and bought two books. I chose an Easy Piano Book and a Fake Book, just as the lessons had suggested.

I went through the Easy Piano Book, learning to sight read without too much difficulty. That was when I began playing songs I had heard all my life. This particular Easy Piano Book was based on Broadway musicals. I knew most of the songs already, so it was great to be able to play them.

The Fake Book, on the other hand, was full of modern pop songs. I had read through the lessons and found out how to use a Fake Book, so I quickly began. I did not know all the chords, so I looked up the new ones before I tried to play each song.

Soon I was playing songs that I had heard on the radio. This was just as fun as the Broadway songs, and my friends seemed to like it even better. It was a lot of fun for everyone, me included.

I am so glad that I took the time to learn the basics of piano playing. I am not a pro by any means. It does not matter to me. I never wanted to take the world by storm. I just wanted to learn something that would make me personally a little happier. And that is just what I did.

KEY SIGNATURE HOLDS THE KEY

It is difficult to talk about keys without some confusion because the physical blocks you strike are called keys. At the same time, it is also necessary to talk about the theoretical keys music is written and played in. For the purposes of this chapter, keys will refer to theoretical keys and not the physical wood piano keys.

Remember the talk about the lounge singer choosing a key in which to sing. Also remember that keys can be major or minor – happy-sounding or gloomy-sounding. There are many factors that determine what makes up the key of the music. They involve theory that is too complex for most beginners.

However, you can learn the key signatures that show what the key usually is. The key signature is a grouping of sharps or flats on the staff at the beginning of a piece of music. There might be no sharps or flats, and if it is a major key, then it is the key of C major.

For the purposes of beginning key signature theory, it is best to begin with major keys. The important thing to learn is what notes to make sharp or flat when you are playing.

Write on a sheet of paper: F-C-G-D-A-E-B. Now draw a box around the G. This is a way to remember the sharps and the major sharp keys. One of the sharp keys is G, which has one sharp, which is F. Another sharp key is D, which has two sharps – F and C. In other words, you start with the box to learn the name of the major key. Then, you count the letters starting with G. The key will have that many sharps in it, and they will start with F.

For the flats, write down: B-E-A-D-G-C-F. This time draw your box around the F. Therefore, the key of F has one flat, which is a B flat. Then, you go back to the beginning for the next one. The key of B flat has two flats, which are B flat and E flat.

Before you begin to play a piece, look for the key signature on the left-hand side of the staff after the clef sign. It will simply show sharp signs on each line or space that corresponds with the notes that should be raised one half step. Or, it will show flat symbols on each line or space that matches the notes that are to be lowered one half step.

One thing to remember is that, ordinarily, the sharps or flats in the key signature are carried throughout the piece. That means that, for the key of F, every time you see a B on the staff, you play a B flat, for example. The flat or sharp signs will not be written beside those notes as long as the key signature is in place.

The key signature can change during the piece at any point. If it does, there will be a new clef sign and a new key signature marked on the staff at that point. Another time you might play something different is if you have an accidental. An accidental is a note that is not ordinarily in the key. A sharp or flat sign will be written by it to tell you what to do.

The Excellent Guide of Learning Piano

As a beginning player, the key signature is really quite simple. Just use it to tell you what notes to play sharp or flat throughout the piece. You can learn more about keys when you have advanced further in your studies of theory.

LEARNING ABOUT CHORDS

If you have sheet music or songbooks to play from, they will likely have chords to play. There are hundreds of possible chords in piano music. There are major and minor chords, diminished chords, inverted chords, augmented chords, and more. Just because there are so many chords to learn, it does not mean you cannot get started on them right away.

The easiest place to begin is with the major chords. To think about chords, you can start by thinking of the scales. You have played a C scale, which has all its notes on white piano keys. You can start with a C major chord. Remember that the scale went up: beginning note- step-step-half step-step-step-step-half step. A chord can have more than three notes in it, but you are going to choose the beginning note, the third note, and the fifth note.

Therefore, you will be playing the beginning note, skip a step, play the next step, skip a half step, and play the next step – one, three, five. If you will look back at Figure A, you can use the Home Keys position for a C major chord. Just put your right thumb on C, your middle finger on 3 which is E, and your pinkie on 5 which is G. Push down all of the keys together. You have just played a C major chord.

You can invert the C major chord for a slightly different sound. All you have to do is to use the same three notes – C, E, G – and play them in different positions. For example, you can play the E and G in the positions they are on in the home keys, but use the C above middle C with them instead of middle C. Try this and make up any variation of the C, E, G combination you can.

Margo Chen

You can make chords from any scale. Just remember the sequence of the scale and choose the first, third, and fifth tone in that scale. There are two other major chords that can be played all on the white keys. They are the F major chord and the G major chord. Now try these chords. Use the one-three-five sequence to make up each chord.

If you analyze the D, E, and A chords, you will see that their simple major chords are not much more difficult. You just have to put the middle finger on the black key for the third tone in the scale. Remember that D flat is the same as C sharp, and so on. This gives you several more chords to choose.

The next three basic major chords are the opposite of the previous three. The D flat, E flat, and A flat chords are such that you put your fingers on the black keys for the one and five positions and on a white key for the third position. When you invert the chord, you will have to remember which keys were originally one, three, and five, just as always.

It is easy to remember that the G flat, also called the F sharp, chord occurs all on the black keys. You will have to work to memorize the B major chord and the B flat major chord, as they are a little different. B goes white for one, black for three, and black for five. B flat is just the opposite, with black for one, and white for three and five.

Minor chords, the serious or gloomy-sounding chords are easy to make as well. For basic minor chords, you only have to lower the third note one half step. You would end up with a C-E flat-G for a minor chord. This goes back to the scale set-up. When you count your steps and half steps, you need to account for the third step being a half step lower. Therefore, you would have beginning note-step-half step-step-step for the first five notes.

You can continue to learn different chords for a long time before you will have mastered them all. Learning chords gives you a way to add fresh new material to your practice and playing. The more you know, the easier it will become for you to play without written music.

Chapter 4 - Understanding Chords and Modification

It is nice when you are able to set the music aside and play any music that you like. It may be difficult to find the sheet music for every song you enjoy. There are two ways to overcome this predicament, and they are related in a way. One is to use a Fake Book, and the other is to learn improvisation techniques.

You can get Fake Books at music stores or by ordering them online. You can also get a version of the same concept when you come across a simple notation of a song. A Fake Book, or the like, has only two things to guide you. First, you will get a melody line in the treble clef. This will usually only show one note at a time – no chords – and it will be a simplified version of the song.

The second thing you will get with this simple music is a letter above the staff. The letter signifies the chord you are to play in the bass clef and possibly add to the treble clef if you are skilled enough. There will be a letter above the staff each time the chord changes.

By learning the chords, you are preparing yourself nicely to be able to use a Fake Book with ease. You can use the straight chords or invert them. You can play them as running chords where you play each note separately in succession. You can come up with any rhythm you choose for the bass clef.

Using a Fake Book is a somewhat creative endeavor. You have to use what you know to fill in the blanks that are left by an incomplete score. In that regard you are in charge of inventing the music. You can find Fake Books that are fairly current, with music you have heard recently on the radio.

Yet, if you want to really come up with your own original song or instrumental piece, you can do it better by learning to improvise. You can learn very complex theory about improvisation, but you can begin with the information you already have. You need to know mainly about scales and chords.

Choose a scale to work from; a C scale may be the easiest for you since it is all on the white keys. Next, choose some chords within that scale. For the C major scale, common chords to use are F major and G major. This is because they do not have any sharps or flats in them.

Make up a chord progression. It can be C-F-G-C. Practice playing these chords with your left hand. The base chords are usually played below middle C, but that is not a rule, by any means. Play them wherever you see fit. Play them as simple triads or invert them. Play them in any sequence. Play until they come naturally.

When you are comfortable with your chord progression, you can begin to improvise a melody. Just play with your right hand, one note at a time to make a melody line. It may not seem like music at first, but if you keep trying you will eventually come up with an interesting melody line.

You can also improvise on a melody you know. Say you want to play Jingle Bells, but you do not have the music. You can quickly pick out the melody. Then, you can choose chords to go with the melody based on the key, or scale, the melody is in. If you do not have sheet music, these are ways to play without it.

Playing Music for the First Time by Sight Reading

Sight-reading written music is when you play music as you see it for the first time. When you first get a piece of sheet music or a new songbook, all the music will be unfamiliar to you. You can get overwhelmed if you try to play perfectly from the very first glance. There are a few tricks you can learn to make it easier.

1. Look at the key signature. This could possibly be the most important piece of preliminary information you can have. Think very hard about which sharps or flats are listed in the key signature. You will want to remember to use those notes whenever they occur throughout the piece.

2. Look at the time signature. The measures will not make much sense to you if you do not know how many beats there are in each one of them. If you do not know what kind of note makes up a beat, you will be lost.

3. Look over the piece for any changes in key signature and time signature. You may be playing along and come across a change out of the blue. If you are not prepared for it, you might end up playing the song incorrectly from that point on.

4. Notice what note you will start on and what note or chord you will end on. It helps to know the starting point and the ending point of any song before you start to play it. This will guide you towards the finish of the song.

5. Glance at the type of rhythm that is used in the left hand. The left hand is usually the rhythm hand, though not always. If you count out the notes of the left hand before you begin, you will have a better idea of how the song is going to go.

6. Do a one-handed once-over of the melody. Just play the melody line by itself to get the sound of it into your mind. Once you know that sound, you have unlocked the uniqueness of the song. When you begin to play the song all together, the melody will stand out in your mind as a significant thread.

7. Look at any other markings that are on the piece. Some of these markings will be covered in Music Terminology. They include the loudness or softness of a piece, how short or long you hold the notes, and the overall speed of the music.

8. Take a deep breath, focus, and begin to play. You should try to play the song all the way through when you sight read it for the first time. There will be time later to break it down into measures and work on each one if that is what you want to do. For the time being, however, just do your best and keep going.

You might wonder why it is important to know how to sight-read in the first place. After all, you could learn the song a little at a time. Sight-reading forces you to keep trying until you reach the end of the song.

When you sight-read properly, you avoid some bad habits. You avoid the habit of looking at each note slowly before you play it. You also avoid the habit of starting and stopping every time something goes the least little bit wrong.

If you want to play perfectly from the very first sight of a song, you might as well forget it unless you are very experienced or talented. Sight-reading gets you started on the road to learning to play better.

Chapter 5 - Piano Language and Terminology

There is so much music terminology for piano players that even experienced players come across new terms on piano music. Some of the words used are more common, though. A few of these are listed for you.

Accelerando – getting faster as the section of the piece marked goes on.

Adagio – played very slowly

Allegro – played at a fast tempo and with a cheerful mood

Andante – played moderately slowly

A tempo – go back to the original tempo

Beat – the basic unit of time in music, it is a regular tap of the foot, for example

Chord – when you play three or more notes together all at once

Coda – an ending that is different than previous verses in the musical piece

Crescendo – getting louder and louder through a marked passage

Diminuendo – getting softer and softer through a marked passage

Dolce – sweetly

Ensemble – a musical group, it could be anything from a band to a classical group

Forte – means to play the piece loudly, forcefully

Fortissimo – play the piece very loudly

Genre – the category of music (or any other artwork), rock and blues are examples

Glissando – playing down the keyboard rapidly, usually by sliding thumb down the keys

Interval – the distance between two musical tones

Largo – very slow and broad

Mezzo forte – play the piece somewhat loudly

Mezzo piano – play the piece somewhat softly

Phrase – a unit of music, denoted by a curved line under or over notes phrased together

Pianissimo – play the piece very softly

Piano – play the piece softly

Presto – play extremely fast

Semitone – also known as a half step

Staccato – play notes quickly, crisply, and detached from each other

Tempo – the rate of speed of the musical piece; it can vary during songs when marked

Variations – when you play a basic tune and then play different versions of it that retain the same basic melody.

These are the most common music words used by pianists, along with the words that have already been used in these lessons. Keys, key signatures, time signatures, notes, whole notes, quarter notes, and so on; improvisation, etc. There are always more words to add to your musical vocabulary.

Some of the words above are written out above or between the staffs. Some are noted by using a mark of some sort. There are many markings to learn, but some of them are easy. This is because the word is often written out along with the marking.

For example, a crescendo marking starts as a point on the left and opens up wider to the right. Sometimes, the word crescendo will also be written somewhere either in the marking or under it to help you. Some markings you will have just have to learn. Staccato music is marked by dots under the notes you are to play short and crisp.

When you learn all of this musical terminology, do not sit back and ignore the rest of the words and markings you find. Keep learning and you will never get bored. There is always more to know.

Choosing Music that is Right for You

You can learn and enjoy yourself by playing music you make up and write, or make up and improvise on the spot. Sooner or later, you will want to find some sheet music or songbooks for more music. You can get music in music stores or online easily, but it may not be the music you want to try and play.

You need to find music that suits your level of play. The best way to do this is to just look at the music. If you are buying in a store, you can examine the books or sheet music thoroughly before you buy.

One thing you can look at is how many sharps or flats the songs in the songbook tend to have. A song that uses too many of the black keys is harder to play when you are first starting out. Also, for some reason, many people find the sharp key signatures more difficult to manage than the flat key signatures.

Look, too, at the difficulty of the chords. If the chords are clusters of many notes, you will know that the chords will not be as easy as simple triads. Take note of whether there are chords of four or five notes together on both left and right hands. You can learn these if you want to, but be prepared to work a little bit.

Look for difficult rhythms. You might see a lot of dotted notes or notes with different values mixed together to make up a measure. Again, you can take your time and learn these songs. You can clap out the rhythms until you have them down before you play. However, if you are looking for some quick success, look for more even and simple note values.

Besides looking at sheet music and songbooks that are already printed, there is another way to buy music in a music store now. Many stores have a special computer set aside for making copies of music. You choose the song you want from a list. If you only know a few words, you may still be able to find the song if the search tools are good enough.

After you have selected your song, you get the opportunity to look at the music. You can look at the music from beginning to end, but you cannot copy it until you agree to buy it. The artists are protected in this way because the store pays the royalties from your payment when you buy the copies. You should expect the copies to be high quality, and on good paper.

You can also get sheet music online. When you buy online, you usually do not get as good of a look at the music you are about to buy. You are more likely to get a small sample to give you an idea of what the music is like.

Margo Chen

The online companies do not like to show too much because it is too easy for people to steal work that is printed on the internet. They will send you your choices by mail or by download as soon as you pay.

No matter how you get your music, be sure that you get the music you like and you will be able to play in the near future. There is no need to stockpile music for that someday when you will suddenly be playing like a pro. Instead, get songbooks and sheet music that you are ready to use right away.

CHAPTER 6- PRACTICE MAKES PERFECT

If you are playing the piano as an adult self-learner, you will do best if you work in some practice time most days. You might like to establish a routine of how you will go about your practice. You can do things in a certain order, or you can mix things up differently every day.

One thing you should always do when you practice is to play scales. You do not have to play every scale every day. You might want to focus on the flat scales one day and the sharp scales the next. You do not even have to take it that far – just be sure that you practice scales of some kind for awhile before you begin to play.

Next, play some chords. Build on the scales you have played and make up as many chords as you can manage in the time you have allotted to spend on the exercise. The more you play your scales and chords, the better you will be when it comes to improvising. You will even play written music better because it will make more sense.

It is a good idea to have a set musical piece to play every time you practice before you start playing other songs. It can be any song that you can play fairly easily. Something that gives you a feeling of satisfaction is always a good choice. Make sure you do not pick a song that is new or tricky for this. You want to start out with a positive experience. You can work on the hard music later in the practice session.

After you have played your starting piece, go on to play songs you have been working on. Go over the rough spots carefully and try to play them from beginning to end without stopping. At this point it is a good time to sight-read any new music you have on hand and want to try. Then, take a little break.

Get a drink of water, eat an apple, or make a phone call. Then, go back to the piano and finish your practice. Many people believe that you have to sit down and play until you are exhausted. They never consider that taking a break can breathe new life into your playing.

Once you have had a break, you can use the rest of the time to improvise. You can make up music based on the chords and scales you played earlier. If you prefer, you can go in a completely new direction. Let this be your time for enjoyment and pure pleasure. With the right attitude, improvisation does not seem like work at all. It feels like complete freedom.

While it is good to practice most days, do not hesitate to take a day off if you are feeling bored with it. There is nothing that kills enthusiasm like overwork. Take off just enough time to renew your excitement about playing the piano. It should not take long.

If you are having trouble finding motivation to practice, go to a piano concert, buy a piano player's CD or MP3 download, or listen to a movie soundtrack based on piano music. Whatever it takes to get you back in the groove, do it.

PLAYING PIANO FOR EVERYONE

You have learned to play some songs very well. Your friends and family are anxious to hear you play. This is no time to disappoint them. Play your heart out and give them a show to remember. There are a few things to consider when you are in this position.

First of all, your friends and family can be your kindest audience or your harshest critics. Most of your loved ones will want you to do well. They might be so careful of your feelings that they tell you how great you played even if you know you made a lot of mistakes.

There is nothing like the loving kindness of a friend or relative. You can become more confident if you know you are going to get praise when you play. However, if the admiration is not sincere, you will feel cheated. You might eventually stop playing for them because it does not seem to matter what you do – you always get the same reaction.

When friends or family members try to help you polish your act, they can be troublesome as well. They might or might not know something about playing the piano. If they know nothing about it, their advice will be nothing more than an irritation and an annoyance. It will not help you in the least when it comes to correcting any mistakes.

If there are other piano players in your intimate circle, they can be demanding. If you play better than they do, they might be jealous. They might say things to demean you. If you are not as advanced as another piano player in the room, you may be up for some pretty harsh criticism. Friends and family members often feel as if they have the right and even the responsibility to set you straight every time you miss the mark.

In the end, you have to play what you enjoy to play and hope that everyone enjoys it as well. You cannot please everyone, nor should you try to. It is far better to play without fear of what others might say than to worry about every little note. Remember that your loved ones generally want what is best for you. They just have a strange way of showing it sometimes.

Choose times to play for your friends and family when music seems a natural part of the occasion. If there is a birthday, ask if the host would like you to go to the piano and play Happy Birthday. For Christmas parties, you can volunteer to play carols for the group to sing. For a casual evening, you might see if people want to hear current songs. It is important to bring the others into the event and let them be a part of it.

When you are playing for a small, casual group such as this, it is good to start a conversation with the others about what they would like to hear. If you know how to play it, or can improvise it, perform it for them right away. If it is something you are unfamiliar with, suggest that one of you looks for the sheet music for a later song fest.

Your friends and family will enjoy your playing if you are committed to making their experiences pleasant or moving. It is also good if you always look for ways to keep your repertoire up to date so that you can surprise and amaze your small audience. After awhile, your loved ones will look forward to hearing you play.

PLAYING FOR THE PUBLIC

If you practice and play long enough, you might get enough experience to play outside your most intimate social circle. You might be asked to play piano for a church service or as a member of a rock band. You might be given the opportunity to play the piano as a paid soloist for a wedding, engagement party, or funeral. There are many chances to play the piano in public if you are someone with reasonable talent and experience.

If you are playing from sheet music, you can make your life easier by preparing your sheet music or songbooks ahead of time. Get some plastic sleeves that you can put a page of music into and place each sheet in a sleeve. If you own a book, you can cut the pages from the book and insert the ones you need into the sleeves. Then, clip the sleeves in order into a ringed binder.

Using a binder makes it easier to turn pages without dropping your sheet music or fumbling with a bulky book. The music is all right there, and you will not damage the corners by trying to turn the pages too quickly. Another advantage of using the binder is that you can put all the written music for the entire performance in one binder. Then, you do not have to keep going from one sheet or book to the next over and over.

The Excellent Guide of Learning Piano

You might get some butterflies in your stomach when you play for a crowd. It is perfectly natural. The main thing to remember is to relax. Tighten up your muscles and then let them go. You will feel a sense of calm after you do this. If the situation is right, you can calm your nerves by talking softly to other musicians while you are waiting for the event to begin or the curtain to go up. Never talk when you will disturb the audience, though.

The most important thing to do when you get nervous is to think about the music. Let your mind drift away from the audience and the circumstances of your playing. If you have chosen your song well, concentrating on the music will carry you through the nervous times. You will not have to do much thinking about the event you are covering because the song will speak for itself.

There are times when you play with other instrumentalists, such as in a rock or country band. You might have written music, but often you will be improvising. Sometimes, you will be trying to imitate someone else's version of the song you are playing. Be sure you know the goals of the group in this regard.

When you are playing with others, do not hog the limelight all the time unless you are the featured player. In most cases, you will be just one member of the ensemble, doing your own individual part to make up a balanced act. Remember to let others have their turns to shine.

If you accompany a chorus, you can lead them to a certain extent. You can set the pace according to the lead of the choral director. On the other hand, if you accompany a solo singer, your job is to provide just a framework for the singer. At the same time, you need to be flexible enough to mold your playing to the variations the singer makes in her performance.

Playing for public events need not be scary. You do not have to be a musical genius to do it either. Just do your best and your experience should see you through.

Chapter 7 - Inspiring Personal Stories

I never dreamed that I could ever play the piano before a group of strangers and sound like anything truly musical. I just learned to play for my own enjoyment. I wanted a pastime that would keep me busy in the evenings while my kids were busy with homework and extra-curricular activities.

I kept practicing and learning more as the months went by. I picked up more and more music books, eagerly poring over every note. The day came when my brother asked me to play the piano for his daughter's birthday party.

I felt like he was only being generous to me. He knew I wanted to play for the family and he was giving me a chance. I was not too nervous because the party for the five-year-old in question would be all family except for a few kids.

What I never thought of was that my cousin would be there – my engaged cousin – my soon to be married cousin. She was looking for someone to play the piano at her wedding. When she heard me play at the party, she decided that she liked my style. She asked me right then and there if I had the date of her wedding open to play piano for her guests.

I was a little shocked. After all, it was to be a very large wedding. I was not an extremely experienced piano player. Surely she could have gotten someone better, I thought. However, she explained that the few people she had considered were unavailable. She was not satisfied with the alternative players she had found, but she really liked my playing. She was serious.

I knew I could not play Mendelssohn's Wedding March. I was just not ready for such an ambitious piece. I could not spread my fingers out so well for such big chords. I was not sure I could play it fast enough either. I asked my cousin about this. She said not to worry. She would just choose another song to leave the altar on.

After much back and forth, my cousin convinced me that I could accomplish what she wanted me to do. I practiced her selections, prepared my music, and got through it nicely when the time came for the wedding. I did so well, in fact, that two other guests came up to me and asked me for my number so that I could play for them.

Oh, and I did learn the Mendelssohn's Wedding March. The more weddings I played for, the more experience I got. With more experience, I learned how to play more difficult songs, and songs like that one were such standards that I had them nearly memorized in no time.

Now, I play for all kinds of public and private events. I have been asked to be one of the regular pianists for my large church. I think I will take them up on it. I enjoy the playing and I can think of no better way to use my gifts. My husband asked me once if I would have rather been a concert pianist. I tell him no. I enjoy playing for the events of everyday life. I bring music to the worlds of people who would never listen to a piano concert. It is more than just a hobby, it is a calling.

CHAPTER 8- TIPS IN PLAYING PIANO FOR BEGINNERS

To get a jump start on learning to play the piano, you can use a few extra tips. Some of them are obvious, but they need to be said anyway. Others, you might not have thought of at all. Keep this list in mind as you start to learn.

1. If you are really not interested in the piano, do yourself and everyone else a favor. Do not try. Maybe you reason that it would be advantageous to play the piano, but your heart is not in it. In that case, you could listen to lots of piano music and see if you develop an interest. Do not start trying to play until you are happy at the thought of learning.

2. Play what you like. In the old days, and often even today, piano teachers spent months with their students before they were allowed to play anything they enjoyed playing. You will get more gratification if you find ways to play at least simple or improvised versions of songs you know and like. That will keep you going.

3. Dive right in. Do not wait for the sun to turn purple or even to learn all the scales. Start playing music as soon as you can. The more you play, the more you will learn. The more you learn, the more you will play. It creates an upward spiral that will increase your abilities.

4. Try to play on the best piano available to you. Of course, you can learn quite a bit with even a small electronic keyboard. If you have a Clavinova it is better because this instrument has all 88 keys. Some would say that an upright piano is better still. Undoubtedly, if you have access to a good grand piano, play it.

5. Do your best not to disturb others in the household. They will almost certainly hear you play. In most houses, there is no getting

around that. Yet, you can be considerate of the times when other members of the household need quiet time to study or do work that is intellectually challenging. Maybe they have had a hard day and just need a little peace. If you ignore their feelings, friction between you will make your practice unpleasant.

6. Set up your own reasonable discipline. Do not be harsh with yourself. If you will not allow yourself to stop a practice no matter what exciting thing is happening in the household, you will come to resent the piano. Allow yourself a little leeway. At the same time, keep up the practice as much as you reasonably can. It is with practice that you will develop your ears, your eyes, your hands, and your mind.

7. Keep a journal of new things you learn. If you come across a new term, look it up either in a music dictionary or on the internet. Write it in a notebook or make a document on your computer to type in all the things you have learned. You can also write in the notebook what has worked for you and what has seemed to make things harder. Do not forget to record your accomplishments.

As a beginning piano player, you have all the time in the world to learn new things abut your instrument. Each time you find something that makes your life easier; remember it so that you can use it again. When you do that, you can build on each lesson and advance to higher and higher levels.

Piano Lessons and Mentor

When you are beginning to learn the piano, you might feel that you need all the help that you can get. You might look for lessons online or through the mail. Getting a piano teacher may be a priority for you. These are possibilities you can consider.There are many different people and companies offering piano lessons online. Some of the lessons are very expensive and some cost less. It may be difficult to find out the price of the lessons without committing to them, but you can do it if you are careful.

You should definitely make sure that you are going to be getting lessons from a reputable teacher. Do not be afraid to ask for qualifications and accomplishments. Some websites offer several free lessons to get you started and give you an idea of what is to come. One website offers over 100 short free lessons before you buy.

Online piano lessons might be helpful to you. The problem is that they are very generic and do not accommodate your own personal learning curve. They are not designed with you in particular in mind. You can get most of the information from reading.

On the other hand, a piano teacher might be more helpful, providing she is a good one. You must expect a lot from a piano teacher. Look for someone who will change her teaching style when her original methods are not helping.

Try to find a teacher who works with scales, chords, and improvisation. More piano teachers are training their students on these subjects now than ever before. Make sure you find one of them, and not someone who sticks to written music alone.

Get a music teacher who plays well herself. Regardless of what has been said about, "Those who cannot do teach," your teacher might be a very able piano player. It is to your advantage if you can find someone who knows the tricks of the trade from experience.

Interview piano teachers to find out which one you might get along with the best. Personalities are important. You will want someone who will inspire you, but not someone who will be unkindly critical. You will want someone you can talk to on an equal level when the subject is not piano playing. After all, you should be given the respect that is due any adult learner.

When you believe you have found a piano teacher who can help you, you can begin your lessons as soon as she can work you into her schedule. Do not leave it at that. Always be aware that you can change piano teachers at any time.

If your piano teacher does not seem to know much about the kind of music you want to play, do not do the easy thing and stay in her lessons. In time you will completely lose interest in playing the piano and quit. Keep searching until you find that special teacher that can help you learn all you want to know.

It might take awhile to find the right piano teacher. In the meantime, you can keep your interest alive by studying the piano on your own. Learn about how to read music, play scales and chords, and improvise. It can only help you when you are ready to learn with formal lessons through a piano teacher.

Chapter 9 - Learning and Enjoying For a Lifetime

Playing the piano is not something you can fully master in a few practice sessions or lessons. Yet, it is enjoyable all along the way if you find ways to keep up the excitement. From the time you begin playing, you never have to quit as long as you can sit up, move your hands, and your mind is still functioning. That is a very long time for most people.

Even if you go for a few years that you do not have a piano for some reason, you can easily take it up again when you have one once more. You might be a little rusty, but you will not be starting over at square one. You will have a vast store of knowledge in your mind to guide you as you refresh your playing skills.

During hectic days, you will find that playing the piano gives your life balance. What is more, you will have a center of peacefulness to your days. Your family will come to understand that you need your time with your piano to concentrate on something completely different than everyday problems.

When your children go off to college, if they have not gone already, you will find yourself spending more time at the piano. You will suddenly have more time to focus on your practice sessions. Your friends and family will notice the improvement and might ask you to play for them frequently.

As your golden years approach, you can revisit songs of your youth by playing them on the piano. It is often easier to find piano music for old songs than to find the recordings. On the other hand, you might want to keep up with the kids and learn all the new songs. The choice is yours and you can spend your time playing whatever you want to play.

The Excellent Guide of Learning Piano

There are few other really interesting and enjoyable hobbies or pastimes you can be involved in during your advancing years. Too many times, older people are given boring tasks or busy work to try to make their days go faster. How much better it is when the elderly can manage their own time with some well-played piano music. It makes them happy, as well as those around them.

No matter how you look at it, the piano learning you begin now is only a prelude to the happiness the pastime will give you in the future. If you keep playing, you will find all sorts of occasions where you can play for fun or profit. If you only play in the privacy of your only home, though, you will get a peace and contentment that is unique to people who find fulfillment in their music.

Therefore, learn all you can and keep your interest alive, but do not feel that the benefits are short-term. Plan to make playing the piano a part of your everyday routine for the rest of your life. You will be pleased that you took the time to find a pastime that offers you so much.

If you have never considered learning to play the piano before, now is a good time to explore the option. It is never too late as long as you have all your faculties intact. However, the longer you have to play, the more you will get out of it. If you are truly interested in playing the piano, do not put it off another day. Start learning all you can from this moment on. It may be the best thing you ever did for yourself.

About The Author

Margo Chen is a professional piano teacher, musician, and author who devoted most of her childhood years playing piano and listening to music. She found herself solidarity by listening into music's rhythm and playing the piano.

She has a gift of learning the sounds of music and really wants to excel and strive to learn more.

She wrote this book to share her knowledge and experience with other people. She set up a mission to inspire more people and help them get a better understanding of music, since she considers the music as food for the soul.

www.ingramcontent.com/pod-product-compliance
Lightning Source LLC
Chambersburg PA
CBHW051028020225
21279CB00017B/348